INVESTIGATING NATURAL DISASTERS

INVESTIGATING
FLOODS

BY ELIZABETH ELKINS

CAPSTONE PRESS
a capstone imprint

Edge Books are published by Capstone Press,
1710 Roe Crest Drive, North Mankato, Minnesota 56003
www.mycapstone.com

Library of Congress Cataloging-in-Publication Data
Cataloging-in-Publication information is on file with the Library of Congress.
ISBN 978-1-5157-4040-7 (library binding)
ISBN 978-1-5157-4112-1 (paperback)
ISBN 978-1-5157-4129-9 (eBook PDF)

Editorial Credits
Alesha Sullivan, editor; Steve Mead, designer; Morgan Walters, media researcher;
Laura Manthe, production specialist

Photo Credits
Capstone Press, 11, 13; Getty Images: Barbara Zanon, 15, Bloomberg, 27; Shutterstock: Danny E Hooks, 12, dcwcreations, middle 29, goir, bottom 29, guentermanaus, 8, ikonacolor, (water vector) Cover, John Williams RUS, (wood texture) Cover, Markus Gebauer, 16, MaxyM, Cover, Nathan Holland, 18, 19, Nik Merkulov, design element throughout, cover, Phil MacD Photography, 5, Ruud Morijn Photographer, 10, Sergey Zaykov, 6 , 7, thomas koch, 20, Vadym Zaitsev, 25, VladimirCeresnak, design element, Volodymyr Krasyuk, top 29, Yanfei Sun, 22

Printed and bound in China.
007883

TABLE OF CONTENTS

WATER, WATER EVERYWHERE

It was December 2015. Heavy rainfalls soaked England, Scotland, Ireland, and Wales. One area received 14.3 inches (36.3 centimeters) of rain in only 24 hours. Thousands of homes were flooded. Bridges were damaged, and in many places travel was disrupted. People fled their homes with the help of the military and lifeboat services.

Defenses, such as sandbags and **barriers**, were put in place to help stop flooding in Cumbria, United Kingdom. But the sandbags and barriers did not keep the water away from homes and businesses. More storms followed all month. The flooding grew even worse as rivers overflowed their banks. More than 20,000 homes across England were left without electricity.

EL NIÑO

Heavy rainfall in the winter is unusual. These rains were partly due to a weather pattern called **El Niño**. This climate cycle raises ocean water temperatures and brings large amounts of rain to different parts of the world. El Niño weather patterns do not happen regularly. They usually occur every two to seven years.

The British Army helped rescue people trapped in their homes from the flooding in the U.K. in 2015.

barrier—a gate used to control the flow of a body of water

El Niño—a complex series of climatic changes affecting the equatorial Pacific region and beyond every few years

FLOOD BASICS

Floods are the most common natural disasters in the world. They threaten lives and property. They cause damage that takes years to fix. And many times people are powerless to stop them.

A flood happens when the ground isn't able to soak up water. The water rises until it is a few inches deep and sometimes many feet deep. Water may arrive suddenly or creep slowly higher. Sometimes the water drains away quickly. Other times an area stays flooded for weeks.

Not every flood is the same. Overbank flooding happens when water from melting snow or a heavy rain overflows the banks of a river. The water creeps up across nearby land. Flash floods send fast-moving water through an area and are very dangerous. These floods happen so fast that there is very little warning. They can be caused by large amounts of rain falling in a short amount of time. This makes fast-moving water rise very quickly. Floods can also be caused by a dam bursting or **levee** failing, sending a huge volume of water downstream in an instant.

Heavy rain in a short period of time can cause dangerous flash flooding.

levee—a bank built up near a river to prevent flooding

Ice jam floods happen in winter when ice forms. Heavy rain pushes chunks of river ice together. They form a dam. Water piles up behind the ice and spills onto nearby land. When the ice breaks up or melts a large amount of water is suddenly released. This causes floods downstream.

A landslide caused by heavy rains destroyed a street in Amazonas, Brazil, in 2008.

Mud from landslides can also cause flooding. Debris from landslides can be carried by water as it flows down a slope. It can pick up trees and the remains of building and bridges. When the material reaches a river, it creates a dam that holds back the water and causes flooding.

Floods can also happen because of big storms. Hurricane Sandy, in 2012, brought so much rain to the New York City area that large parts of the city were flooded. The subway tunnels and coastal parts of the city were underwater.

CAUSES OF FLOODS

▶ Melting snow causes a river to rise steadily. The water overflows its banks, creeping into nearby fields and homes.

▶ Heavy rainfall makes a river rise quickly, sending a surge of water pouring down a hillside.

▶ A dam breaks and releases the water it had been holding.

▶ A hurricane or strong storm pushes water onto the coast.

▶ A large amount of rain falls onto dry, hard soil and cannot be absorbed.

▶ Heavy rainfall brings more water than a city's sewer system can carry away. The flood fills city streets, and water may flow into people's yards and homes.

WHERE DO FLOODS HAPPEN?

Floods can occur almost anywhere. **Floodplains** are important. They provide a place for water to go when snow melts or heavy rain falls. This water helps carry nutrients to the floodplain's soil. The nutrients make it easier for plants to grow. Floods can also help control **erosion**. When floodwaters spread over a large area, the water flows slower than it would if it was in a narrow riverbed. Less soil is worn away from riverbanks when water moves slowly.

A floodplain is generally a flat area of land near a stream or river.

Floods can affect buildings constructed on floodplains. These are the areas around rivers where water overflows during a flood. The area closest to the river is called the floodway. The water here will probably be flowing when a flood occurs. The area at the edge of the floodplain is called the floodway fringe. The fringe area might have standing water during a flood. Floodplains are a natural way to handle excess water. But when people build homes too close to a floodplain, the homes are at risk of flooding.

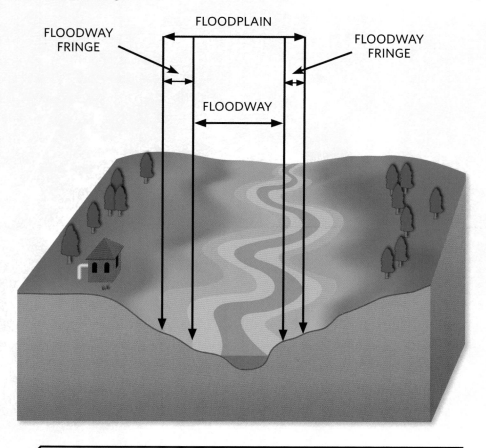

FLOODWAY FRINGE

FLOODPLAIN

FLOODWAY FRINGE

FLOODWAY

floodplain—an area of low land near a stream or river that becomes flooded during heavy rains

erosion—the wearing away of land by water or wind

Areas that receive heavy rainfall experience more flooding. The country of Bangladesh in South Asia receives heavy rainfall during the **monsoon** season. This is the most flood-prone area in the world. On the other hand, places that are usually dry, such as deserts or regions that do not receive regular rainfall, often flood because of storms. If the ground is very dry and hard, rainwater cannot soak in. Instead rain runs across the surface and can cause flash floods.

FLOODS AND WILDLIFE

Flooded areas are important resting places for animals. Birds flying north or south stop in flooded fields and wetlands to eat. In 2010 an oil spill in the Gulf of Mexico endangered many birds that lived in the marshes off the coast. Farmers in the state of Louisiana were asked to purposely flood fields so birds would have places to rest and find food.

Places that get a lot of snow in the winter may have floods when the snow melts in the spring. Melting snow causes river levels to rise. Spring rains also bring more water to rivers and may cause riverbanks to overflow.

Coastal cities are often affected by hurricanes. These storms bring heavy rains and may also cause a storm surge. This happens when winds push water toward the shore. A storm surge creates higher sea levels, which move inland and cause flooding.

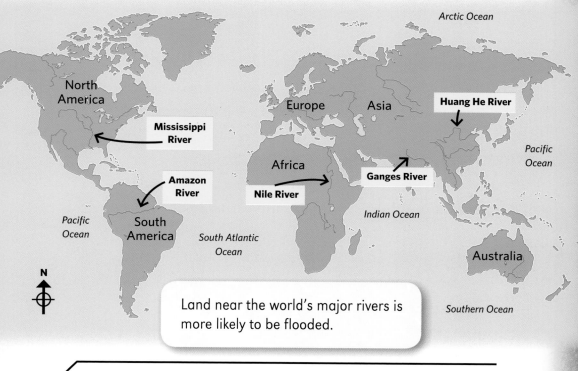

Land near the world's major rivers is more likely to be flooded.

monsoon—a very strong seasonal wind that brings heavy rains and hot, dry weather

Some cities that are in danger of flooding have built a system of huge gates that can be raised and lowered when high water threatens the area. London, England, and Venice, Italy, are two cities where high water levels often create flooding. London built gates on the Thames River called the Thames Barrier. The gates can be raised and lowered when the river's level rises. This controls the amount of water flowing into nearby rivers. Venice is in the building stages of constructing MOSE, which stands for Modulo Sperimentale Elettromeccanico. MOSE is a system of flap gates that will raise and lower where the city's **lagoon** meets the sea. The gates will hold back the high tides that bring floodwater into the city's canals.

Researchers are also working on a high-tech system that uses environmental data from **satellites**, weather balloons, and computer models to predict flood risks. Satellite images show forecasters where clouds and heavy rain may be present. Weather balloons carry instruments that measure wind speed, air pressure, and temperature. Computer simulations use information on wind speed and air pressure to create models. The models show which areas may experience storms in the days ahead. The data collected from this technology can help predict storms and floods. Giving people early warning about floods will provide more time for evacuation and may prevent flood-related deaths.

The MOSE project in Italy is intended to protect Venice from high waters and flooding.

FACT

The city of Venice experiences *acqua alta*, meaning high water, often in the winter. It is a very high tide that floods the city's canals, squares, and walkways.

lagoon—a shallow pool of seawater separated from the sea by a narrow strip of land

satellite—a spacecraft that circles Earth; satellites gather and send information

AFTERMATH

The damage from floods can be extensive and long-lasting. Floods can be deadly. Thousands of people around the world die in floods each year. Floods can also leave behind extensive damage. Buildings and cars are often washed away. Vehicles that have been covered in water are often too damaged to repair. Roads are washed out, and pavement buckles and cracks. Bridges may be swept away. If floodwater covers farm fields, crops are often destroyed.

A house stands alone in a flooded area in Australia in 2011.

FACT

By the year 2050, flood damage in the U.S. is expected to cost $1 trillion a year, mostly due to climate change and coastal city flooding.

Homes that are still standing after a flood may be permanently damaged. Floodwaters can soak mattresses and furniture. Carpets and floors may be wet or coated with mud. The flood may have carried **sewage** into the house. The home's **foundation** could be ruined, making the home unsafe. Even after cleanup, mold may grow in walls and insulation and make people sick.

When a dam holding back iron-mining waste burst in Mariana, Brazil, in 2015, a flood of thick, red, toxic mud smothered the town. The flood flattened buildings and trees and killed people and animals. Drinking water was polluted, and rivers were filled with red **sludge**. Wildlife was killed. It will take a very long time for the environment to recover.

sewage—liquid and solid waste that is carried away in sewers and drains

foundation—a solid structure on which a building is built

sludge—a wet, muddy mixture

THE WORST FLOODS IN THE WORLD

One of the worst floods in the U.S. took place on May 31, 1889, in Johnstown, Pennsylvania. A dam on the Little Conemaugh River broke, sending 20 million tons (18 million metric tons) of water moving at 40 miles (64 kilometers) per hour. It rushed 14 miles (23 km) downhill into Johnstown with no warning. More than 2,200 people died, and some of their bodies were never found. Property damages reached more than $17 million.

Hurricane Katrina hit the city of New Orleans, Louisiana, on August 28, 2005. The storm caused massive flooding when the levees that held back the waters of Lake Pontchartrain were damaged or swept away. Floodwaters poured into the city. In some areas people had to scramble into attics and onto rooftops to escape the rising water. More than 80 percent of the city was underwater. Almost 2,000 people died, and there was more than $100 billion in damage.

Flooding caused by Hurricane Katrina was one of the United States' most expensive natural disasters in history.

The flooding in Pakistan in 2010 destroyed thousands of people's homes and businesses.

The Indus River in Pakistan flooded in 2010. The monsoon rains there had released a record amount of rainfall. Some parts of the country in the northern mountains experienced flash floods. These floodwaters then moved downriver, sweeping away roads and bridges. Large areas of farmland were underwater. The contaminated floodwaters made drinking water unsafe and destroyed food crops. More than 2,000 people died, and millions more suffered from homelessness, disease, and starvation.

The United Kingdom suffered severe flooding in 2012. In North Wales the River Elwy rose to 14 feet (4.3 meters), which is twice its usual level. An elderly woman drowned when she was unable to get out of her house as it filled with water. Volunteers worked day and night using boats to ferry people from their homes to dry ground. People trapped on an island had to be rescued by aircraft. Over 500 homes were evacuated. Even with these valiant efforts, five people died.

Flooding in 2009 caused by the high river level of the Huang He in South China destroyed homes and businesses.

In 2004 Indonesia suffered widespread flooding from a tsunami after an earthquake struck. A tsunami is a huge wave or series of waves caused by the movement of the ocean floor from an earthquake. Waves more than 100 feet (30 m) high brought massive amounts of water onto the land. Trees and buildings were flattened. People were swept away and drowned. Witnesses say the waves sounded like a freight train. Huge tsunami waves hit coastal areas all around the Indian Ocean, killing more than 230,000 people in 14 countries. It was the worst flooding disaster in recent history.

The Huang He River in China has flooded many times in the last 150 years. Researchers estimate a total of 7 million people have died from the Huang He flooding or from food shortages when crops have been destroyed. The Huang He usually floods because **silt** is deposited in the riverbed. The silt raises the river level until the water overflows its banks. Thousands of miles surrounding the river are then covered in water. Many dams have been built to help control the flooding.

FACT

The 2004 tsunami in Indonesia killed many people but spared others. A lucky baby was found floating in the floodwaters on a mattress, alive and well.

silt—small particles of soil that settle at the bottom of a river, lake, or ocean

A CHANGING CLIMATE

Flooding is expected to happen more frequently in the future because of climate change. The amount of rain that falls during the heaviest downpours is increasing as the average temperature is increasing in some regions. This is because warmer air holds more moisture than colder air. If the temperatures around the world continue to increase, scientists predict that rainfall may also increase by as much as 40 percent. More rainfall will mean more flooding. Higher sea levels will also bring more flooding to coastal areas.

Humans often make choices that increase the chances of their homes flooding. People are building homes and other structures on floodplains, so when rivers rise, the chances of flooding are greater. People are also paving over more of the landscape for roads and parking lots. Paved surfaces do not absorb water. When there is a heavy downpour, the water has to flow to unpaved areas, which can cause flooding.

FACT

Climate change is also causing bigger blizzards. This simply means that heavy precipitation is falling as snow in the winter instead of as rain in warmer weather.

Climate change may bring increased precipitation to many parts of the globe.

MANAGING FLOODS

It might seem that there is very little that can be done to avoid flooding. But experts are working to reduce floods and the damage they cause. Scientists in Japan have designed a system of huge underground tanks. Rainwater from rivers and **channels** flows into these tanks. Then the water is safely pumped into other rivers that are located away from the center of cities. The huge pumps can release the equivalent of a swimming pool's worth of water every second.

PREVENTATIVE MEASURES

Some engineering practices can help prevent floods from getting out of control. Parking lots paved with a special type of concrete that water can seep through are less likely to flood. Rain gardens are dips in the land, planted with shrubs, flowers, and bushes. When water fills the dip, it holds the water as the plants soak up the excess through their roots. A retention basin, also called a flood pond, is a dry area meant to contain extra water during a storm. These ponds are usually located next to rivers, streams, and lakes.

channel—a narrow stretch of water between two areas of land

The Metropolitan Area Outer Underground Discharge Channel, an underground tank, in Kasukabe City, Japan, helps protect the city against flooding.

Another important tool experts use to manage floods is a river gage. Gages measure the depth of rivers and how fast water is flowing. A river gage records data every 15 to 60 minutes. The data lets weather forecasters know which rivers are at, or near, flood stage. The forecasters can then warn people to get out of an area before a flood becomes dangerous.

STAYING SAFE

There are many things you can do to make sure you and your family stay safe during flooding. Here is a helpful list of dos and don'ts:

✔ DO:

Listen to local weather and emergency broadcasts. They will issue flood warnings that tell you to evacuate to higher ground.

If a flood happens, move to higher ground and stay away from flooded areas.

If you can't get out of your house, move to the top floor, attic, or roof.

Keep a battery-powered radio on hand to listen to news reports and alerts.

If you are traveling, avoid places that might flood, such as canyons or floodplains.

✘ DON'T:

Do not drive into flooded areas. Roads may have collapsed, the water might be deeper than it looks, or your car could be swept away.

Do not wade into a flowing stream that reaches past your ankles. Even flowing water beneath knee-level can knock you off your feet.

Do not swim or play in floodwater. It may be contaminated.

Do not camp near rivers or streams.

Do not touch any electrical equipment if you are standing in water.

FLOOD EMERGENCY KIT

It is a good idea to make an emergency kit for bad weather. It will help you be prepared in any disaster. It should include:

- **a battery-powered flashlight or lantern**

- **a battery-powered radio**

- **extra batteries**

- **drinking water**

- **food that will not go bad, such as canned goods (don't forget the can opener) or boxed snacks**

- **first aid supplies**

FIRST AID KIT

GLOSSARY

barrier (BAR-ee-uhr)—a gate used to control the flow of a body of water

channel (CHAN-uhl)—a narrow stretch of water between two areas of land

El Niño (EL NEEN-yo)—a complex series of climatic changes affecting the equatorial Pacific region and beyond every few years

erosion (i-ROH-zhuhn)—the wearing away of land by water or wind

floodplain (FLUD-plane)—an area of low land near a stream or river that becomes flooded during heavy rains

foundation (foun-DAY-shuhn)—a solid structure on which a building is built

lagoon (luh-GOON)—a shallow pool of seawater separated from the sea by a narrow strip of land

levee (LEV-ee)—a bank built up near a river to prevent flooding

monsoon (mon-SOON)—a very strong seasonal wind that brings heavy rains and hot, dry weather

satellite (SAT-uh-lite)—a spacecraft that circles Earth; satellites gather and send information

sewage (SOO-ij)—liquid and solid waste that is carried away in sewers and drains

silt (SILT)—small particles of soil that settle at the bottom of a river, lake, or ocean

sludge (SLUHJ)—a wet, muddy mixture

READ MORE

Dougherty, Terri. *The Worst Floods of All Time.* Epic Disasters. North Mankato, Minn.: Capstone Press, 2012.

Linde, Barbara M. *When Floods Flow.* Eye on the Sky. New York: Gareth Stevens Publishing, 2016.

Marquardt, Meg. *The Science of a Flood.* Disaster Science. Ann Arbor, Mich.: Cherry Lake Publishing, 2016.

INTERNET SITES

FactHound offers a safe, fun way to find Internet sites related to this book. All of the sites on FactHound have been researched by our staff.

Here's all you do:

Visit *www.facthound.com*

Type in this code: 9781515740407

Check out projects, games and lots more at
www.capstonekids.com

CRITICAL THINKING USING THE COMMON CORE

1. Why can large amounts of rain actually be dangerous in a very dry place? (Key Ideas and Details)

2. What are some things that humans are doing that can cause floods and increase flood damage? (Key Ideas and Details)

3. What are some things that you and your family can do to prepare for a flood? (Integration of Knowledge and Ideas)

INDEX